Come Closer to Me, God!

Donald L. Deffner

Publishing House
St. Louis

PHOTO CREDITS: Robert Holland—p. 57; Walter Moll—p. 45; Joan E. Rahn—pp. 28, 36; Bruce Roberts—cover, pp. 17, 63, 76; Louis C. Williams—p. 88.

Manufactured in the United States of America

Library of Congress Cataloging in Publication Data

Deffner, Donald L.
    Come closer to me, God!

    1. Christian life—Lutheran authors. I. Title.
BV4501.2.D424   248.4'841   81-22107
ISBN 0-570-03851-0 (pbk.)   AACR2

---

1 2 3 4 5 6 7 8 9 10 PP 91 90 89 88 87 86 85 84 83 82

To my wife,
Corinne

Author's Preface

In an earlier volume, *You Promised Me, God!* I noted that often the Christian feels that God is silent or isn't even there any longer. But the God who has made nearly 9,000 promises to us in the Bible *is* there. And our real problem is that we fail to trust His promises. (See James 2:4.)

Yet our faith is not only in the promises but especially in the Promiser. And so we need to search the Scriptures again and again to come to know our great God better. As we do, the Holy Spirit guides us to learn how to pray, how to live, and how to die.

Bryan Green once said that the only truly private thing one can do is to die. All the rest of our life is lived in community, and every action we take has social significance. Accordingly, as I composed this sequel volume to *You Promised Me, God!* I was quite conscious of the need for a more corporate approach to the trials, the challenges, and the ambiguities of life. The whole volume could have been written: *You Promised Us, God!*—where the "Us" would be myself and those with whom I relate: the church and the world—global concerns, world hunger, racism, justice, peace, etc. A number of the vignettes do grapple with those crucial areas of involvement with others in the Christian's social responsibility.

But beyond the fact that a host of books are available which deal with those issues today, I still felt one's own life needs to be in proper perspective before going out to change the world. And so this volume primarily continues to examine the struggle of the individual Christian seeking to be in a right relationship with God.

In the following vignettes I have again sought to be faithful to the nature of God as revealed in the Old and New

5

Testaments. Each piece is based on Scripture passages listed in the order they are alluded to in the vignette. Where a number (1) appears with a vignette, it corresponds to the author listed at the end who is to be credited for the statement(s) or germinal idea behind the piece.

May the Holy Spirit bless your meditation on these promises—and in this book, loving challenges—from our Lord, that you may grow stronger in reliance on the One who made them—the Promiser Himself.

How This Book Can Be Used

Each of us finds that God fulfills His promises to us in different ways. But we can still share that experience with others and encourage those needing help to search the Scriptures and hear the voice of a loving Father talking to His beloved children.

This could be done in small groups where a vignette is read, after which the Scripture passages are examined in a variety of translations. Then individuals might share ways in which a particular promise or challenge of God has been evidenced in his or her life.

And then . . . why not write some yourself?

Contents

THE CHRISTIAN ASKS—
Why are You testing me, God?
GOD RESPONDS—

Blossoms in the Desert

Nothing but sunshine
makes a desert
While the rain
makes it bloom
Are you willing
for Me to send
a few clouds
your way
That the flowers
of My love
may blossom
in your life?

2 Corinthians 12:9

Stormy Weather

Just as a tree
is buffeted
twisted turned
stretched and bent
in a storm
So I am going to
buffet you
stretch you
so your roots
will be forced
to go deeper

into the subsoil
of My strength
I know
it will hurt
But I only
test those
whom
I love
And that includes
all
of
My children

Hebrews 12:6

Expect the Unexpected

Don't get used to
the ordinary
the routine
For I have a way
of jolting you
at times
Learn how to
expect the unexpected
Pain
for example
My testing
So that you may experience
My love
and My healing
For without testing
there is no freedom
But also there is
the unexpected challenge
of a new enterprise
a gift

a release
a blessing
Expect those
unexpected things also
In the Name
of the Father
and of the Son
and of the
Holy Surprises

Psalm 27:14   *Isaiah 40:31*

Tennis, Anyone?

The person
unfamiliar with tennis
saw the ball
hit the net
repeatedly
and wondered
why they didn't
take down the net
As you know
it was there
to test
the players' ability
and improve their skill
So don't complain
when I put up the nets
in your life
They are not there
to impede you
but to
improve you

Isaiah 48:10   *Zechariah 13:9*
Malachi 3:2

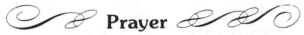 **Prayer**

Give me the precious insight of recognizing Your hand in my times of testing, Lord. By Your grace, give me the power to withstand temptation and not to fall. And help me always to remember that the purpose of my trial is to realize my need to lean more fully on You, my strength and my shield. In the strong name of Jesus Christ. Amen.

THE CHRISTIAN ASKS—
Why am I so depressed, God?
GOD RESPONDS—

That Depressing Rain

I saw you sitting there
gloomy depressed
because of the interminable rain
I was depressed too
when My people let Me down
and I let it rain 40 days and 40 nights
But another time I let it rain in Germany
and My child Luther reminded his people
that it was raining
corn wheat barley wine
cabbage onions grass and milk
All our goods we get for nothing he said
And he added
"And God sends His only-begotten Son
and we crucify Him"
So you think you're depressed?
Count your blessings
For all that is Mine
I have given
to you

Genesis 8:22   *Philippians 4:11*
1 Timothy 6:8

Moody?

Some people
down there
think a clever author

has just discovered
the secret
of overcoming
depression
Actually he rediscovered
an old truth
of Mine
The secret is that
your mood need not
decree your thinking
Rather your thoughts
control your moods
I say
if you think right
you will feel right
Ponder that
for a time
And the key
as to what
to think about?
I care
for you

Philippians 4:8

Sex

You say
you are sexually frustrated
and are jealous of
the affectional fulfillment
you see others have
and which you feel I have denied you?
Take heart
It is not a sin
to be tempted
but to yield to temptation

So although you cannot
keep the birds
from flying over your head
you can keep them
from making nests
in your hair
And I the Lord
promise you the power
to be faithful
to Me

1 Peter 2:11   *Romans 6:13*
James 4:7

Lonely/Alone

You think *you* are
lonely?
alone?
Can you imagine
My loneliness
when I created a person
in love
gave so much
to that beloved child
of Mine
and then
My beloved lives
and spends each day
as if
I don't exist?
That hurts
You think *you* are
lonely?
Seek Me
and you will
find me

In fact we shall
find
each other!

Proverbs 8:17

That Haunting Calvary Cry

You say you're depressed?
How do you think I felt
the day My Son
died on Calvary?
Can you imagine
the grievings in My Spirit
when I heard His cry
that I had forsaken Him?
You say you're depressed?
You are not alone
But remember Easter!
Joy!
Victory!
And because He lives
now you can live
and without
depression

Ephesians 4:30

 **Prayer**

Forgive me, Lord, for wallowing in self-pity when I should be basking in the warmth of Your love. Please send Your Holy Spirit to me to guide my thoughts—that my mood may change, and my whole being might exult in praising You, the only Source of my peace and strength. In the strong name of Jesus Christ. Amen.

THE CHRISTIAN ASKS—
How can I get to know You better, God?
GOD RESPONDS—

Why, Lord?

You ask why
your friend is not healed
Why a healthy life and body
is being wasted
And Christians have prayed
and nothing has happened
And they are baffled
in the light of My promises
But remember
I am the Lord
There are times
you need reminding
Who I am
I know you are disheartened
I call you to trust Me
Recall what I have
done for you
I gave you My only Son
Forgiveness
Calvary
Easter morning
And one day you'll see Me
face to face
And then
you won't have any
questions

Job 13:15   Jeremiah 29:13
Romans 11:33-36   1 Corinthians 13:12

I Am like the Ocean

I am like the ocean
At times I am quiet
At other times
turbulent
I am vast
And no one
can fully
fathom Me
But I also have
great riches
still untapped
Hidden depths
of My love
as yet unexplored
Search Me
and see
You can discover
treasures undreamed of
For the map is
My Word

Acts 17:11

Just for You

Even if you have not seen
the teeming millions
of Asia
at times you
must have been impressed
by hordes of people
pushing past you
in a crowd
Do you realize

I know the number
of hairs on each person's head?
But more
realize
that My Son
didn't just die
for crowds of people
which He did
but for every individual
who ever lived
no matter how evil
or ignominious
or ugly
or unlovable
Pick a person out
in that crowd
and consciously think
of My Son's dying
for that one individual
And then concentrate
on the fact
He died
just for you

Matthew 10:30   John 3:16   Luke 23:39-43
1 Corinthians 15:13

Have a Good Flight!

So you enjoy
a safe flight
in an airplane
And you commend
the pilot
and the aircraft's inventors
and the skill
of many others

Guess who
made it all
possible?
Underneath you
are
the everlasting arms
and they
are Mine!

Deuteronomy 33:27

Are You Thinking of Moving?

If you think
I am farther away
from you
than I was
in the past
Just make sure
which one
of the two
of us
moved

Psalm 34:18   Psalm 145:18   Isaiah 55:6

The Spectacles of the Spirit

So your friend's
eyes were checked
and they found
glaucoma?
How recently
have you thanked Me
for the gift
of sight?

But there is
a more
precious gift
The eyes of faith
The spectacles
of the Spirit
Learning to walk
not by sight
but by faith
Let Me give you
those glasses

1 Corinthians 2:14   *1 Corinthians 2:9*
1 Corinthians 13:12   *2 Corinthians 4:17-18*
2 Corinthians 5:7

Cecil B. DeMille's
"The Ten Commandments"

I heard that a young woman
down there
saw all those old
Cecil B. DeMille movies
about Bible times
And then she discovered
that popular view
of Christianity
had nothing to do
with *real* Christianity
at all
That's good she said
But she was still amazed
that even through
"all the junk
in those movies"
she saw

My love coming through
A love she never knew
existed
A sacrificial love
through My Son Jesus
Whom I gave
to you
You know
I can show up
in the
strangest
places[1]

Exodus 20:6

 **Prayer**

When I don't understand You, Lord, please help me to put my hand on my lips, like Job. Give me the grace to be still and expectant in Your presence. Help me to realize that Your silence is not evidence of Your absence. And grant me the wisdom to wait on Your own timing for the renewal of my strength. In the strong name of Jesus Christ. Amen.

THE CHRISTIAN ASKS—
How can I get along better with others, God?
GOD RESPONDS—

Pluralism

You say you fear
the person you work with
who is always
putting you down?
You say you can accept
that person's different opinion
but yours is never respected?
Take heart
Which one of you two
is the one most
dogmatic
opinionated doctrinnaire?
Be patient
I know what's going on
You are not alone
Be patient
with that other person
Keep on doing your own thing
Or better yet
Do My thing
in your own way

Psalm 27:1   *Numbers 14:9*   *Psalm 23:4*

Friends

Have you thanked Me lately
for My gift of friends?

Friends to whom you can turn
in time of need
Whom you can trust
cry and rejoice with
And yet sometimes
your closest friends
can disappoint you
I want you to know
I am your Best Friend
I will never
let you down

John 15:14

A Third Dimension

Your relationship
with any person
a friend
a lover
a person in your family
is not a matter
of your being loved
Of course you need that
But more
It isn't even
your loving the
other person
That's of course
crucial
But it's
even more
It's your catching
My vision
of what
that other person
can become

through My indwelling
My presence
My power
Now that's
a challenge
Are you willing
to free your friend
from your grasp
to be
what I want
your friend
to be?[2]
1 Corinthians 7:22

Revenge!

So you think
you would really
like
to get even
with
that person
Oh how
you would
enjoy it
But vengeance
is Mine
I can
handle that person
And by the way
thinking about you
Are there any times
in your life
when *you*
have wanted
My mercy

rather than
My judgment?

Romans 12:19

Breathe Deeply

My children!
Have you considered recently
how interdependent
all of you
are on each other?
For food clothing
shelter travel
a thousand
daily needs
But I
am still
the Source
of it all
Your very next breath
comes from My Spirit
Breathe deeply
You can depend
on Me

Genesis 2:7   Psalm 104:30

A Failure to Communicate

So you say
you just can't communicate
with that person
anymore
I'm sorry
But there is One
with whom

you can always talk
Me
Search My Word
and you will hear
My voice
Speak to Me
and while you
are still talking
I will answer
Come
Let us
communicate
with each other

Psalm 120:1   *Isaiah 65:24*

I'm Sorry

If you can't learn
to say
"I'm sorry"
to those you hurt
especially those
you love
most of all
then I am sorry
for you
For I challenge you
Repent
and change
or you won't
be forgiven
by Me
And One Day
up here
when you say to Me
"Lord! Lord!"

I'll say
"I'm sorry"

1 John 1:8-9 *Matthew 5:23-26* *Matthew 7:21*

Like Stars in the Sky

I challenge you
with My Promise
Does your life in Christ
make you strong?
Does My Son's love comfort you?
Are you kind and compassionate
to others?
Or are you selfishly ambitious?
Do you have a cheap desire
to boast?
Or like My Son
are you humble
and looking out for other people
and not just for yourself?
I challenge you
Have the mind of My Son
That of a servant
Humility
Obedience
Even to death on a cross
for you
So don't complain or argue
Be innocent and pure
in a world of crooked and mean people
Shine among them like stars in the sky
And then One Day
I will smile on you
My child
That's a promise!

Philippians 2

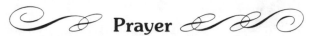 **Prayer**

Please help me to appreciate Your gift of my friends, Lord. But even more, help me to *be* a friend to the friendless. Move me to reach out of my shell to the lonely, the depressed, and yes, especially the loveless. And keep me ever mindful of the One Friend who will never let me down. You, Lord. In the strong name of Jesus Christ. Amen.

THE CHRISTIAN ASKS—

How can I get rid of my guilt, God?

GOD RESPONDS—

The Sin Against the Holy Ghost

I understand
you are disturbed
about whether
you have committed
the sin against
the Holy Ghost
of which
My Scriptures speak
and for which
there is
no forgiveness
Be calm
That sin involves
hardness of heart
And the fact
that you are
concerned
means that you
haven't committed
that sin
Be calm
And keep the channels
open
to be a receiver
of My Spirit

Mark 3:28-29   *Ephesians 4:30*   *John 16:24*
Galatians 3:14

The Woman in Red

If you never have
been guilty of
infidelity
in your life
just remember
Who protected you
from yourself
and don't be proud
Now on the other hand
if you *have* fallen
take heart
Remember My Son's friend
dressed in red
He didn't put her down
But forgave her
So I say too
I love you
If you are
truly sorry
I forgive you
Just
don't
do it
again

Matthew 7:1   *John 8:1-11*

Hate/Love

You've heard people
say
that hate is very close
to love
especially for

married people
I'm different
I've never hated you
I get angry
with you at times
and justifiably so
But you are My child
Just know I
detest your sin
But still love you
the sinner
And I still love you
when you go astray

Ezekiel 33:11   *Romans 6:1*   *Mark 10:21*

Feeling Guilty

You say
you feel guilty?
Know this
My Son not only
took your guilt
upon Himself on Calvary
but He *felt*
the guilt also
your guilt
Remember His cry
of pain while dying
But recall also
His promise to
the penitent thief
Today
you will
be with Me
in Paradise!

2 Corinthians 5:19-21   *John 17:4*   *John 19:30*

You're Just like Adam and Eve

You seem
to have a way
of committing
the original sin
over and over again
every day
just like Adam
and Eve
However
there is forgiveness
with Me
every day
Just don't
take it lightly
If you are truly sorry
I forgive
But don't just sin
that My grace may abound
I'm not just
in the business
of forgiving
I also
call to account

*Psalm 130:4   Romans 6:1   1 John 1:8-9
Matthew 25:41-46*

 **Prayer**

Keep me tuned in to the right channel, Lord. Help me
to be a receiver of Your Spirit. And that I may not grieve
Your Spirit, please save me in the time of trial that I may not
sin. And when I fall, grant me a truly penitent heart, that I
may not take Your grace lightly. In the strong name of Jesus
Christ. Amen.

THE CHRISTIAN ASKS—
Why am I hurting, God?
GOD RESPONDS—

The Burden Relieved

I can feel the weight
of your burden today
For I live in you
Why not let
Me be
your burden-bearer?
The difficult thing
I know
is to truly
and fully
let go
But I dare you
And I will empower you
to release that anxiety fully
to Me
And you will find
relief
Cast your cares
upon Me
I have broad shoulders
and long arms
which are at once
underneath you
and outstretched
on a cross

1 John 4:16-17   *Psalm 55:22*
Matthew 11:28-30

You Hurt Me!

You were hurt
when your friend
made that cutting remark
And now you are
nursing your wound
alone
Or was there some truth
in the remark
And the real problem is
self-pity?
I know hurt also
Learn from Me
to be forgiving
when others hurt you
And by the way
Did you ever hear
of God
pouting?

Psalm 42:5

A Friend of Pain

I heard someone
down there say
you should
"make a friend of pain"
That's intriguing
I can see the point
of being ready for
the pain
and coping with it
And I do send it
to those I love

at times
to show them
I am still
testing them
as My children
But don't welcome pain
as your real friend
For I am your True Friend
and I only permit pain
occasionally
to bring us closer
together

Hebrews 12:6-8

The Promise Beyond the Pain

You cannot
manufacture joy
but I can
give it to you
sometimes
in strange ways
For example
through pain
Not that you should
seek suffering
or wallow in pain
But when your defenses
have been
painfully destroyed
Then in retrospect
you will see
that pain
has taught you
something
which pleasure

cannot
So don't court pain
but learn from it
The blessings
it can produce
Like My son
dying
on a cross[3]

Romans 5:3-5   *Hebrews 12:7*

 **Prayer**

Help me to see Your promise beyond my pain, Lord. Move me to stop depending on myself and instead to look to You for healing and comfort. When I hurt, please keep my mind fixed on Him who suffered the greatest pain of all—Your Son, my Savior Jesus Christ. In His strong name I pray. Amen.

THE CHRISTIAN ASKS—
How can I grow in my faith, God?
GOD RESPONDS—

I Like to Watch You Grow

You say you
like to see things grow?
I do too
It was My power
that planted you
in your mother's womb
I love nourishing you
and watching you grow
One day you
will be
put in the ground
like a seed
But My Son
who was in the
ground
for three days
and then sprang to life
will call you
to burst forth
and you will
blossom
in My gardens
here
forever

John 1:3   *Job 31:15*
Psalm 22:9-10   *Psalm 71:6*
Psalm 139:13-14   *John 14:19*
John 14:2

A Young Girl Crying

I saw a young girl crying
Because her mother
who was always traveling
sent her many presents
But the girl cried
"I don't want them
Mother
I only want *you!*"
That's the way
I feel
about you
Don't give Me
your half-hearted promises
Even your tithe
doesn't impress Me
if it doesn't come
from your heart
I don't want
things
I want
you

Joel 2:13

Going It Alone?

Don't always try
to go it alone
For two are better
than one
When two work together
you will find fulfillment
and rejoice
When two work together

if one of you falls
the other will lift you up
And if someone attacks you
you have better defense
A threefold cord
is not quickly broken
So don't
always try
to go it alone
And by the way
I would like to be
your partner

Ecclesiastes 4:9-12

Don't Worry

Don't worry
about anything
Instead pray to Me
for what you need
And don't forget
to thank Me
for My answers
And when you do this
you will experience
My peace
which is more wonderful
than any human
can understand
And My peace
will keep your thoughts
and your heart
quiet and at rest
as you trust in My Son
Christ Jesus

Philippians 4:6-7

 Prayer

Lord, let me accept the fact that my groaning pains are really growing pains and that You are putting me under pressure that I might better fit the mold You prepared for me from eternity. Bend me, shape me, use me, Lord! But please fill me with Your Spirit. I know I cannot do it alone. I open myself to You, Lord. In the strong name of Jesus Christ. Amen.

THE CHRISTIAN ASKS—
How can I face death, God?
GOD RESPONDS—

Proud and High in the Water

You think your friend
is dead and gone?
In one sense you are wrong
For though you saw that friend
on the shore of life
like a vessel
with a full head of sail
and then that ship
moved farther away until
it was only a speck
on the horizon
and then vanished
I from the other shore
saw that speck become
a full-masted vessel again
proud and high in the water
Now berthed here in My harbor
together we look forward
to the day
when another vessel appears
on the horizon
Yours

1 Corinthians 13:12

Numbers Don't Count

I saw your shock
at the small turnout

at your friend's funeral
But there was another death
My Son's
And not too many people
showed up for that
He was despised
and rejected
But your friend
was not
I was
at both funerals
And remember
I know
the qualities
of your beloved
Christian friend
So worry not
about numbers
They don't count

Isaiah 53:3   *Hebrews 13:5*

Untimely Death

Your friend died unexpectedly
But know that
I did not
"call your friend home"
as some say
Death comes
to all
For all
have sinned
Now I must say
I knew the time
But
I didn't will

your friend's death
Death is
your enemy
and Mine
Know this
Short-lived
as that person's life was
Which would you choose?
To have that friend
with you
for a short
space of time
or not
at all?

Romans 5:12

When Will You Die?

One of My children
down there
when asked
how he approached
his death
said he didn't fear it
but he wasn't
yearning for it
He was living
joyfully
each day
for itself
That's a good balance
Is it
yours?

Philippians 1:23

Your Friend Died?

You say you miss
your friend who died?
Remember I did too
during that
person's absence
from My presence
here in the home palace
But you should see
your friend now
happily going around
shaking hands
with old friends
and making new ones
Like Peter and Paul and John
Mary and Elizabeth and Dorcas
and countless more
I'm sorry you hurt
But remember
Your friend is *beyond*
all pain and loss
In perfect peace
with Me
So grieve not
as those who have
no hope
But rejoice for the gladness
your loved one now enjoys
And remember
soon
soon
we will share it
together

Isaiah 26:3   *1 Thessalonians 4:13*
John 14:2-4

The Dark Bedroom

Do not fear death
For just as a parent
calms a child
frightened by a darkened bedroom
So I say to you
Come
Take My hand
Let's go in
Together

John 14:19

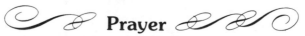 **Prayer**

My heart is heavy, Lord. My pain is indescribable! But I know *You* can understand it. I miss my loved one, Lord! Help me, help me, please, to realize that my loved one is at peace in Your presence. Give me, by the grace of Your Holy Spirit, the ability to remember the blessings from You which we both shared. And give me, I pray, the balance of a life that continues to do Your will here and now but which joyously awaits The Day when we'll both be reunited together with You. In the strong name of Jesus Christ. Amen.

THE CHRISTIAN ASKS—
How can I serve You better, God?
GOD RESPONDS—

Busy! Busy!

I know you are
very busy
I have been
impressed by your schedule
But do you have the time
for common things?
Like
taking that widowed person
to the doctor?
Or spending time
with a parent-less child?
Or just listening
to a lonely person
talk?
My Son
took time
with individuals
He never complained
when the lowest
of the low
needed Him
I care
very much
for
ordinary people
just like
you

Mark 10:21   *1 Peter 5:7*

My Feet Are Hurting

I heard about
an impoverished boy
in South America
who had no shoes
And a man
said to him
If there is a God
why doesn't He
love you enough
to give you
a pair of shoes?
And the boy said
God does love me
And He did tell a Christian
to give me
a pair of shoes
But
the Christian
forgot

Matthew 5:42   *Luke 6:38*

The Steward's Ship

You are a steward
of the ship
of your life
I will ask for
an accounting
of your stewardship
when you reach
My shores
A rich spiritual cargo
I hope

For if they ask
when you die
"How much did that person leave?"
The answer will be
"Everything!"

Matthew 6:19-20

Prayer

Lord, please give me a keen sensitivity to the needs of others. In Your infinite love, grant me the power to love my neighbor as myself. Make me an open and an active listener, Lord. Enable me to give of my self in the ordinary tasks when the opportunity to serve others comes my way. In fact, Lord, help me create the opportunity! Give me patience and insight into ways I can give my life for others. As You have given Yourself for me. In the strong name of Jesus Christ. Amen.

THE CHRISTIAN ASKS—
Where are You, God?
GOD RESPONDS—

Silence!

I saw that poster
in your room
which said
It often shows
a fine command
of language
to say nothing
That's true
There are times
you need to
place your hand
on your lips
like Job
and be silent
There are times
you do not hear Me
But I am there
waiting for you
to listen
and to be
a receiver
of My Spirit

Job 40:4   Psalm 46:10

Hovering

I'm always
watching over you

Like a helicopter
high above a train
rounding curves
on a mountain
I can see
where you have been
where you are now
and what's ahead
So don't be afraid
For I know
what's around
the next corner
in your life
No need to fear
I am near

Psalm 121

He Knows

Since I know
each blade of grass
each hair of your head
every grain of sand
in all the oceans
of My world
Since I know
when every sparrow
falls
I also know
what's happening to you
the crown
of My creation
And My knowing
means
My caring

and My caring
means
I am always present
with you
wherever
you
are

Matthew 10:29-31   *Matthew 28:20*

Footprints in the Sand

You doubted Me
You recalled I promised
My footprints would always be
beside yours
in the sands of time
And then you thought
in your lowest and saddest times
you saw only one set
of footprints on the sand
Your own
and that I
had deserted you
My child
My beloved child!
That one set of footprints
was not yours
but Mine
That was when
I
was
carrying
you

Matthew 28:20   *Isaiah 53:4*

I Will Tell You a Mystery!

Now I will tell you
a mystery
When you believe in Me
and that's a gift which
My Holy Spirit
will give you
freely
Then I assure you
of My
love concern compassion
and presence
in a fantastic way
so that even though
I am not speaking
you will know
I am there
and that I care for you
So remember
You may feel lonely
at times
But you are
never alone

1 Timothy 3:9   2 Timothy 1:6
Ephesians 2:8-10   Hebrews 13:5

 **Prayer**

Grant me, O most holy and infinite God, a spark of Your divine insight that reminds me always that Your seeming "absence" is a sign of Your acting. That Your not speaking is nevertheless a sign of Your *being there.* That in Your apparent lack of response to my cries I still am in Your presence. And that in Your Word I continue forever to have Your promises. But even more—You, the Promiser. In the strong name of Jesus Christ. Amen.

THE CHRISTIAN ASKS—
Do I really need the church, God?
GOD RESPONDS—

First Church of the Rock

You know what
one of My most
incredible
promises was
besides sending My Son?
It was when I told Peter
he was a rock
and I was going to
build My church
on a
faith
like his
Well isn't that
one of the most amazing
promises I ever made?
Think of how My children
behaved over the centuries
their failures
to distinguish themselves
from non-Christians
My church goes on
Christianity is not just another
new religion
of the first century
It lasts
And so
do I

Matthew 16:18-19

So You Skipped Church?

So you skipped church?
I can understand that
I've observed many
boring rites of worship
from the jot and tittle
legalisms of My Son's day
to today:
Tedium
rather than
Te Deum
But have you ever tried
to really hear My Word
through a weak vessel
of Mine?
For what you can do
in spite of
the barriers
to communication
is listen for
My Voice
coming through it all
I once heard of a woman
who came to know Me
in a church
even though the sermon there
didn't talk about Me
But she had
listened
to the readings
from
the Bible

Matthew 23:23-24   *Hebrews 4:12*
Isaiah 55:11

Church Walls Don't Make a Christian

Do you know
what your chief activity
will be
when you
are here
with Me?
Worship!
That being the case
you'd better get
going on it
now
I know
church walls
don't make
a Christian
But surely
you can find
some place
to
practice

Hebrews 10:25

Solo Flight?

You and I
have talked
with each other
alone together
quite a lot
But your relationship
with Me

cannot be
a solo trip
For life with Me
and in Me
must be expressed
in community
with other Christians
and in
My Holy Communion
together
You need them
They need you
You can't be
a Christian
in a vacuum

Hebrews 10:25   *1 Corinthians 11:23 ff.*

The Death in the Church

You say that you
look forward to
a life of love
with the saints above
in all the purest glory
but living with
the saints below
is quite another story?
My Son had
the same experience
He knew the pain
of dealing with
His people
on earth
It was part
of the "death"
the New Testament

speaks about
I know that
some of My children
can drive you
up the wall
But if My Son
could live with them
and love them
Can't you?[1]

Isaiah 53:3   *Matthew 22:39*

Prayer

Lord, I keep looking for the perfect church down here, but I am constantly disappointed. Maybe I'm searching for the wrong thing. Please guide me to a fellowship where I cannot *be* served, but serve. Where I cannot only be listened *to,* but listen. Where I can be a giver, but most of all a receiver—of Your Word and Sacrament. Help me to realize my need for others, Lord. And to give of my self in community to others. As you gave Yourself to me. Indeed, to all of *us.* In the strong name of Jesus Christ. Amen.

THE CHRISTIAN ASKS—
How can I pray, God?
GOD RESPONDS

Have a Refreshing Vacation

Don't feel guilty
when you are on vacation
I want you
to work
while it is day
For a day is coming
when you won't work
any longer
My Son
went to weddings
and He also
took time
to rest
and to pray
He spent time alone
on the mountain
in meditation
But then
He went back
down again
to the plain
refreshed

John 9:4

Cry in the Night

In your pain
and frustration

you cried out
to Me
for help
You even admitted
you had been
ignoring Me
You even admitted
you didn't deserve
My help
But you knew
I had never
let you down
And you still
felt free
to cry
to Me
I like that
The trouble is
I came through
again
with My help
But I haven't heard
a word from you
since

Psalm 50:15

Forgotten My Address?

I've been waiting
for a message
from you
for a
long time
I promise
Before you call

I will answer
And while you
are still speaking
I will hear
Try Me
and see

Isaiah 65:24   *Jeremiah 33:3*
Psalm 91:15

The Right Answer

Again you say
I am silent
I am not talking to you
It is not that
I am ignoring you
or that My answer is not
on its way
but
what I am going to say
is not the answer
you want to hear
So think again
Read My Word
and see
if I am not
trying to reach you
after all
Which answer
do you really want?
Your answer
Or My answer?

John 8:31   *Acts 17:11*
Matthew 26:39

Prayer

Lord, teach me how to pray. Open. Expectant. *Believing!* Not trying to bend Your will to mine, but always open to Your grand design. And then *thankful.* For whatever answer You give. In the name of the almighty Father, and the strong name of His Son Jesus Christ, and in the blessed name of the Holy Spirit. Amen.

THE CHRISTIAN ASKS—
God, how can I cope with The Enemy?
GOD RESPONDS—
I Have the Word from the Lord

Don't ever think
you have some kind of
unique
hot line
direct connection
with Me
unlike others
In a sense you do
But only through
the Means
of My grace
The Bible
Your Baptism
The Holy Eucharist
Hearing My Word
Often I have acted directly
Like knocking Paul down
on the road to Damascus
But when I speak to you
It's through My channels
So be careful
When you think you have
"the word from the Lord"
Unless you are hooked up
to My Means of Grace
It could be
a "word"
from someone else

John 8:31-32

The Real Reason

Did you ever realize
that the reason
you are having
such a bad time
is not because
I am punishing you
but because
Satan is tempting you
trying to get you
into his kingdom
because you have
such a potential
for Mine?

Hebrews 12:6-8   1 Peter 5:8

The Rose and the Thorn

Don't think
that everything
delicious and delightful
is necessarily the temptation
of The Evil One
or that the most beautiful rose
has the most piercing thorn
and in order to pluck it
you must bleed
For I want you to enjoy
the precious gifts
of My creation
in accordance with
My Holy Word
So don't punish yourself
with a false self-denial

but savor My blessings
knowing that My Son
has already bled
for you

Genesis 1:31   *Psalm 34:8*

Prayer

Lord, help me recognize the *Real* Enemy. Not just His Satanic Majesty, but *myself*. Make me aware of the evil within me. But also grant me, by the grace of Your Holy Spirit, the ability to resist the Destroyer, the Prince of Liars. Please give me the power of Your Word which Your Son used when He said "Get behind Me, Satan!" That's my prayer too, Lord. In the strong name of Jesus Christ. Amen.

THE CHRISTIAN ASKS—
Why am I so low, God?
GOD RESPONDS—

Self-Pity

Don't court
depression
or self-inflicted pain
For that is
masochism
and I will not
countenance that
in you
Self-pity
is only a luxury
for the indolent
Get your mind
off of yourself
Think on Me
Praise Me
Praise Me
Praise Me
And your lethargy
self-pity
and depression
will fade away
Just praise Me
and see

Psalm 42:11   *Psalms 145—150*

Down Again!

So you are
lonely again

Hear My words
Know I am God
Give thanks to Me
Avoid self-pity
Accept your loneliness
Look who's talking to you!
You are not alone!
Offer your loneliness
up to Me
Do something
for somebody else
And you'll be surprised
at what
will happen[4]

Psalm 46:1   Isaiah 58:10-12

The Well of Loneliness

When you are lonely
Think of being
not in a pit
but a well
My Son
was in the pits
of hell
not to suffer
but to announce
His victory
on Calvary
over the powers
of hell
So drink of the water
of the well
of your loneliness
knowing that My Son
The Living Water

has been there
before you
Lonely on Calvary
victorious
in hell
announcing
the redemption
which now
is yours[5]

1 Peter 3:19   John 4:14

Oh, to be Young Again!

You miss
your youth
and envy
the vibrant young
around you?
Count your blessings
Are you still
young in heart?
You *can* be
Remember many
younger than you
wish they had
your maturity
your achievements
your freedoms
Count your blessings
and remember
you will never
grow old
with Me

Job 11:15 ff.   Psalm 39:5

Prayer

Lord, please get Your Holy Spirit going to thrust me out of myself to help others when I am "in the pits." Do it, Lord! Move me, Lord! Change me, Lord! Forgive me, most of all, for my self-centeredness and self-pity. I call on Your name, O Lord, for You have promised to hear me. And now, I *trust* You. I'm ready, Lord. I am waiting for You, Lord. In the strong name of Jesus Christ. Amen.

THE CHRISTIAN ASKS—
Tell me more about Yourself, God!
GOD RESPONDS—

Good News—Not Bad

Know this
The pronouncement
of My law
My judgment
on your sin
is not
to damn you
but that you will see
the need
for My mercy
I don't desire
your death
but your life
Not your fear
at hearing
My judgment
But your
joy at hearing
My loving
forgiveness

1 Timothy 2:4   Ezekiel 33:11
2 Peter 3:9   Romans 2:4

Sweet Potatoes in Hell

A missionary in New Guinea
told the natives
that if they didn't

believe his message
they would burn in hell
like the sweet potatoes
he had just
tossed into the fire
Their "conversion"
lasted a few fear-filled years
A different missionary
told them about My creating
a beautiful world
I a loving Father
wanted the best
for My children
And then when they
misused My blessings
I sent My Son
who made things
right again
through His death
and resurrection
And when the natives
heard that story
they believed
and for more
than just
a few years

1 John 4:18   John 3:16

The Wrong Choice

I created you
a free person
But there is
no freedom
without responsibility
Adam and Eve

did not live up to
that responsibility
They failed the test
Now I knew
what they would do
But don't blame Me
I didn't *plan*
their choice
I freed them
The origin of sin
was the wrong choice
of a free
moral agent
Freedom!
Do you really want it?
I even
free you
to reject Me
Now that's
real freedom
and
real love[6]

Genesis 3   John 8:36

My Divine Rationale

I am
from eternity
And I am love
So I created
someone to love
You
You have often
spurned this love
and disobeyed Me
your Creator

That requires punishment
Justice
But I still love you
So let Me tell you
a story
I sent My Son
He absorbed the punishment
For you
But at the same time
fulfilled My love
Isn't that fantastic?
Justice and mercy
fulfilled
at the same time![6]

Genesis 1:31   1 Peter 2:24

That's Incredible!

Try to define
time
You can't
Nor can you
comprehend
eternity
or infinity
That's what My love
is like
Boundless
Endless
Matchless
Eternal
Unending
Incomparable
And My love
is yours
forever

Unconditionally
Immeasurably
Unceasingly
Can you ask
for anything
more?

John 15:13   Revelation 1:8
Ephesians 2:8-10

Misunderstanding

So you think
there is a misunderstanding
between you and Me
Well there is not
For I understand you
I know
how I feel
about you
I think
of peace
not of evil
It takes two
to argue
And I'm not fighting
with you
So come
Let us reason together
Search My Word
to hear My voice
And then will come
the peace
that passes
all understanding

Jeremiah 29:11   Isaiah 1:18   John 5:39
Philippians 4:7

Prayer

Lord, help me to understand Your true nature, and not just my wish-projection of You. Drive me back again and again to rediscover the real YOU in Your Holy Word, and as revealed in the life, death, and resurrection of Your Son and our Savior Jesus Christ. And help me, by the power of Your Holy Spirit, in meeting Christ, to see in Him the one I am to be—a "little Christ"—and the power to be that new creation. In the strong name of Jesus Christ. Amen.

THE CHRISTIAN ASKS—
Am I too overconfident, God?
GOD RESPONDS—

Overconfidence

Have you ever noticed
how often
My children fail?
How even a person
you thought so much of
did a horrible thing?
You were disappointed
I was too
And you wondered
whom you could ever
really count on any more
to be trustworthy
Well you can always
count on Me
I will never
disappoint you
leave you or
forsake you
I also give you
My grace
to withstand temptation
But don't become
overconfident
Guess whom
I am watching
right now?
You!

Hebrews 13:5   *1 Corinthians 10:12*
1 Corinthians 16:13

Temptation

You haven't decided yet
Whether or not to yield
to the temptation
But don't think
you can simply sin
and then be forgiven
Oh I will forgive
if you are truly sorry
But don't
take My grace lightly
Play with Me
once too often
and your heart
will harden
Meanwhile
not having yielded as yet
to the temptation
resist it
and enjoy
the double blessing
of My strength
and then
My peace

1 Corinthians 10:13   James 4:7
John 14:27   Romans 5:3-5

My "Trip"

I hear you
have just had
a very
self-satisfying
experience
But tell Me

as Your best friend
Why wasn't I
invited?

Psalm 90:14   *Psalm 91:14-16*

Know Yourself

I see
you have
a very impressive record
accolades
from people
everywhere
But what
do you really
think
of yourself?

Proverbs 29:23   *2 Timothy 2:15*

Taken for Granted

Don't ever take Me
for granted
You've come
to a plateau
and things look
pretty good
You were down
for a time
and called to Me
for help
and I answered you
But now you are
self-satisfied
Don't ever
take Me

for granted
My grace
is not cheap
It cost Me
My Son
So rejoice
in your breathing spell
But be ready
for My next
loving test
It will come
inevitably
For
after every mountain
there is
a valley

Romans 6:1   Hebrews 12:6 ff.   1 Corinthians 10:12

Check Your Investments

As a squirrel
lays up nuts
for the winter
What are you
laying up
for the long
dark night
of the soul?
Listen to Me
stranger pilgrim
in the world
Check what you
have stored up
Will it last?

Matthew 6:19-21   Matthew 19:21

The Wicked Prosper

You wonder why
the wicked prosper
and why
they don't
seem to suffer
like you do
and why
I don't punish them?
Don't worry
They will receive
their reward
I am the Lord
I am not mocked
Meanwhile
How are *you* doing?

Psalm 94:3   *Galatians 6:7*
1 Corinthians 10:12

 **Prayer**

Lord, help me to grow in *Your* confidence in me while I
have less and less "confidence in me." Let me be Your
loved, baptized, forgiven, and always-cared-for child. What
a God You are! *Now* have confidence in me—that I will love
You, serve, and obey You. And this is most certainly true. I
love You, God! In the strong name of Jesus. Amen.

THE CHRISTIAN ASKS—
What else do I need to hear from You, God?
GOD RESPONDS—

The Source of Satisfaction

I have promised
I will meet
all your needs
But in My own way
and at My own time
I hear
some of your
non-Christian friends
are quite amused
that you seek fulfillment
in following their excesses
Does that mean
I don't really
satisfy?

John 2:4   John 6:27
Jeremiah 31:14   Philippians 4:19

My Name

I hear
My Son's name
being used down there
quite a lot
But often as a curse
That's wrong
Another mistake

some will make
will be to call Me
Lord Lord
on the Last Day
but only those
will enter My presence
who have done My will
Now My Old Testament children
never even spoke
My name
because I am so holy
But I give you
a new covenant
I love you
so much
you may
call Me
Father

Exodus 20:7   *Matthew 7:21*
Matthew 6:9

The Decade

A woman was asked
why I gave you
the Ten Commandments
And she said
I must have
loved you
an awful lot
to do so
because
I gave them to you
to protect you
from yourself
That was

a very good
answer

Exodus 20:1-17   *Psalm 119:127*
1 John 5:3

On Public Speaking

You are edgy
about that talk
you are going to make
before a large group
of people?
Don't worry
For you are not speaking
to a lot of people
but to one person
For every person hears you
as an individual
And don't forget
there is also
One Individual
beside you
on the platform
Me
Invisible but supportive
So be prepared
Do the best you can
And we'll do a fine job
together

Psalm 37:28   *Hebrews 13:5*

The Password

I saw Peter
welcoming the new arrival

at the Heavenly Gates
and the newcomer
was exhilarated
to have finally made it
But Peter said
"What's the password?"
The dismayed newcomer responded
"The just shall live by faith"?
"God is love"?
"There is no longer any condemnation
to them that are in Christ Jesus"?
"All those are true sayings"
said Peter
"But they are not the words
which I await to hear
today"
"I give up"
said the man
"That's it!
Come on in!"
said Peter

John 15:5

The Bottom Line

The other day
one of my daughters
down there said
she could take
and even forgive
her husband's
drinking
infidelity
loss of job
and a few other things

But what she
could not take
was the fact
that he
had
lied
to
her
That struck Me
as being
quite
basic
You know
I have never lied
to you

Colossians 3:9

Clever!

I see
you have
all those
clever programs
going which
really meet
your needs
By the way
What have you
done lately
for someone
other
than
yourself?

Isaiah 58:10-12   *Matthew 22:39*

That Fantastic Mockingbird!

Even as the mockingbird
trills his tune
in a thousand
different ways
So My ways with you
are many and varied
Expect the unexpected
Learn patience
flexibility
Learn how to
bend with the winds
of My testing
so you will not break
Let My will
not your will
be done
And know this
Though your life may change
drastically
through My ingenious plan
for you
My care
and love
for you
are
Changeless

Malachi 3:6

Footprints in the Valley

By now you have heard
many of My promises
(there are many more)

and have responded
in faith
feeling you have done
your part
and that now the next move
is up to Me
You are mistaken
You can't fly across
the valley of the shadow
you must walk
the rocky path
step by step
But you are not alone
on your journey
There are always footprints
ahead of you
in the valley of the shadow
They are Mine
Come
let's walk
together[7]

Psalm 23:4

Prayer

I'm keeping myself tuned to Your wavelength now, God. Please don't let the static of my own desires get in the way of Your plans for me. Use me for *Your* kingdom and *Your* purposes. Test me, as You must *(I know!),* but fill me, I pray, with Your Holy Spirit, that I may do Your will, and not mine, O Lord! In the strong name of Jesus Christ! Amen!

AND GOD SAYS—
Go in Peace
Serve Me
YOU ARE FREE!

Credits

1. Edward A. Rauff, *Why People Join the Church* (Washington, D.C.: Glenmary Research Center, 1979), pp. 12—121.
2. Peter A. Bertocci, "What Makes a Christian Home?" (*The Christian Century,* May 6, 1959).
3. Robert M. Herhold, *The Promise Beyond the Pain* (Nashville, Tenn.: Abingdon Press, 1979), pp. 9—10.
4. Elisabeth Elliot, "The Ones Who Are Left" (*Christianity Today,* Feb. 27, 1976), pp. 7—9.
5. Terry Allen Moe, "The Paradox of Loneliness" (*LCA Partners,* April, 1980), pp. 16—17, 37.
6. Leander S. Keyser, *A Philosophy of Christianity* (Burlington, Iowa: Lutheran Literary Board, 1928); and *A System of Christian Evidence* (Burlington, Iowa: Lutheran Literary Board, 1942).
7. Catherine Marshall, *To Live Again* (New York: Avon Books, 1972), p. 113. Reprinted from *You Promised Me, God!,* by the author (St. Louis: Concordia Publishing House, 1981) p. 100.